Recapture Your Finances

Finally!! An easy-to-grasp financial book for all ages and comprehension!

Bina Artiste, professional business owner and accountant

Copyright © 2021 by Bina Chauhan. 806051

All rights reserved. No part of this book may be reproduced or transmitted in any form or by any means, electronic or mechanical, including photocopying, recording, or by any information storage and retrieval system, without permission in writing from the copyright owner.

To order additional copies of this book, contact:
Xlibris
844-714-8691
www.Xlibris.com
Orders@Xlibris.com

ISBN:	Softcover	978-1-7960-7414-7
	Hardcover	978-1-7960-7415-4
	EBook	978-1-7960-7413-0

Print information available on the last page

Rev. date: 12/30/2020

Recapture Your Finances

By Bina Artiste

Proof-read by Tommy Harcus

Dedicated to...

My father, my mother, my sister,

my brother, Tommy,

and Nermall Allan Em.

Book Cover: Made by Bina Artiste using the Canva app

Other Books to Read:

Debt-Free Forever by Gail-Vaz Oxlade (January 3, 2012)

[2014 AuthorHouse.com] Treasures Of Light & Darkness by Bina Artiste Chauhan

[2015 AuthorHouse.com] Of Jewels and Gems by Bina Artiste Chauhan

[2019 AuthorHouse.com] Sliver Moon by Olivia South

[2019 AuthorHouse.com] Gr0und Zer0 by Bina Artiste

[2019 Xlibris.com] F.R.E.E. by Bina Artiste

[2020 Xlibris.com] Recapture Your Finances by Bina Artiste

They say to save while young... Any age is good to save.

How?! You might ask?!

Let me skip the boring introduction and skip the boring chapters, and dive right in. Here are financial secrets I have learned by trial and error, by being a professional accountant in my field, a business owner of YFL – Youth For Life, and hefty amount of budgeting. I started budgeting anally ever since I rented my first bachelor apartment at 25 in the heart of downtown Vancouver, BC, Canada on Nelson and Denman.

Here is a small example of a budget I do every cheque I get, be it big or small. (I use the Notes app on my Iphone.)

Budget - September 20, 2020

2000.00	CERB
200.00	RRSP (10%)
50.00	Emergency Fund (TFSA)
122.47	Virgin Mobile
591.42	Amex Credit Card
10.24	Visa Credit Card
600.00	3D printer/supplies
59.85	Avon business expense
100.00	Furniture
40.00	Dress
100.00	RDSP's

CERB

Registered Retirement Savings Plan (RRSP's) are a good stable locked-in long-term way to save. With the economy being unstable all the time, we cannot rely on the government with Old Age Pensions (OAP).

Credit Cards

At one point I ended up with 5 credit cards and managed to pay off 4 and close the accounts. Now I only have a Visa that I manage. I love this Visa because I accumulate points and every 5000 points I get $50 towards RRSP's. I put on as much money as I can after everything else is paid off.

In Order

First comes 10% RRSP's (pay yourself first) then comes Rent, Bills, RDSP's then Visa. Then I am free to spend it on whatever I want like food and clothing. I do not have children except two lovely cats.

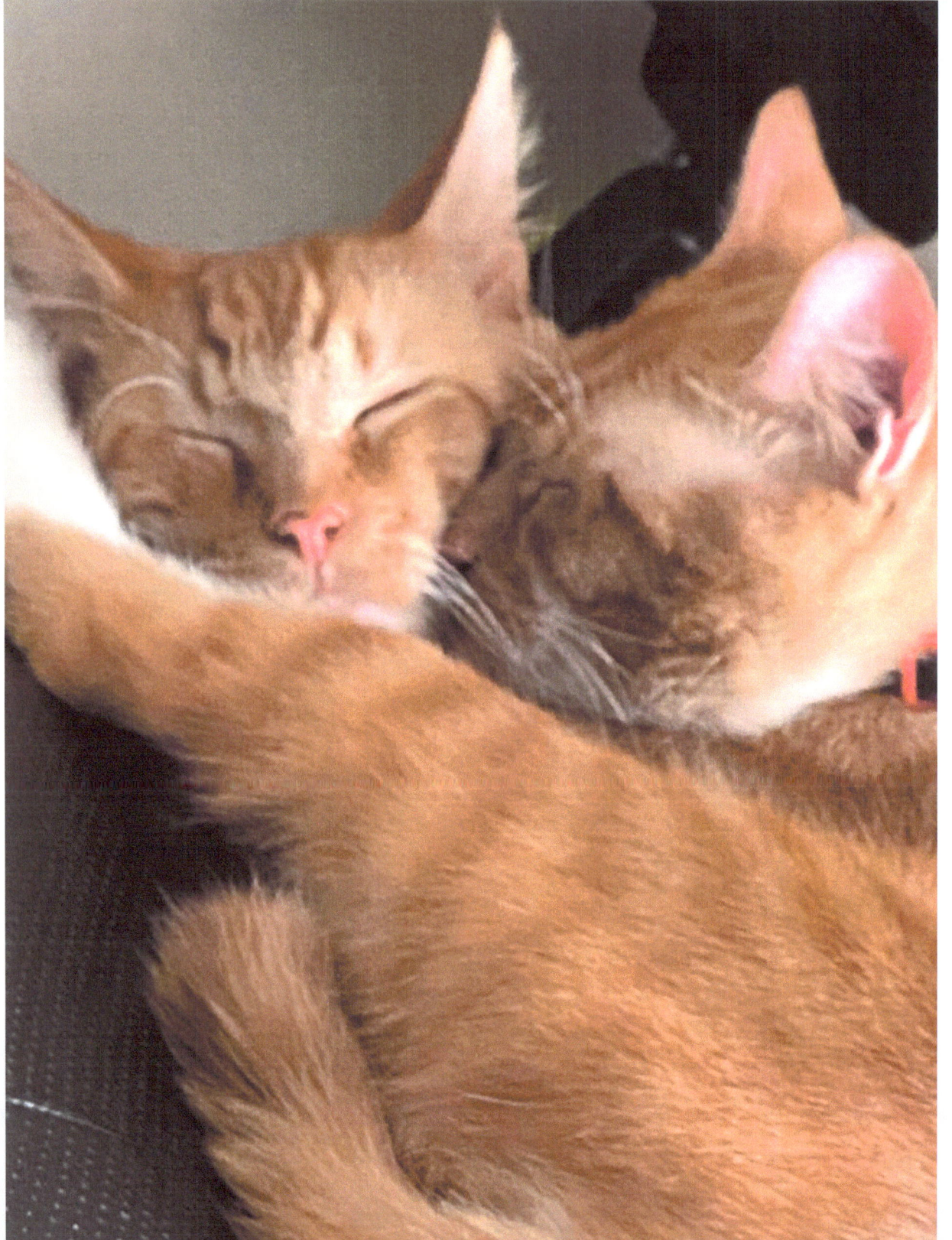

Business

One great way to make money is to start up your own business. I started with Avon Canada because a friend was selling it and she stopped so I joined online and ever since then it's been almost perfect.

I say almost, because my eldest sister purchased $5000 worth of products, after I signed her up, from me. Then she lost her job and didn't pay me. My business almost went under, but I had good support to write it off my taxes as a loss, and my best sister forced evil sister to pay me back. I also lost my leadership status since all my sign-up leads quit. It's better not to do business with family. Needless to say she's banned from the family.

But other than that I have been able to write off all my receipts for the year 100%.

Any groceries goes to meals & entertainment, along with cigarettes and liquor.

I registered my business with CRA (Canada Revenue Agency) as Youth For Life. So I brand everything YFL.

RDSP's

RDSP's, or better known as Registered Disability Savings Plan, is available at a starting $11,000 from the government of Canada, if you are on PWD persons with disability income. Every dollar you invest into your RDSP fund, the government matches times 3. You can invest and contribute until you are 49, and the money is accessible when you are 59.

Budget Jan 20, 2021

1233.42 PWD income

125.00 RRSP

375.00 Rent Subsidy

50.00 Emergency Fund

47.00 Dental Cleaning after Blue Cross

200.00 Braces (Invisalign)

50.00 disability bus pass

80.00 car insurance

306.00 Visa credit card

This time I am going to put it into a pie chart:

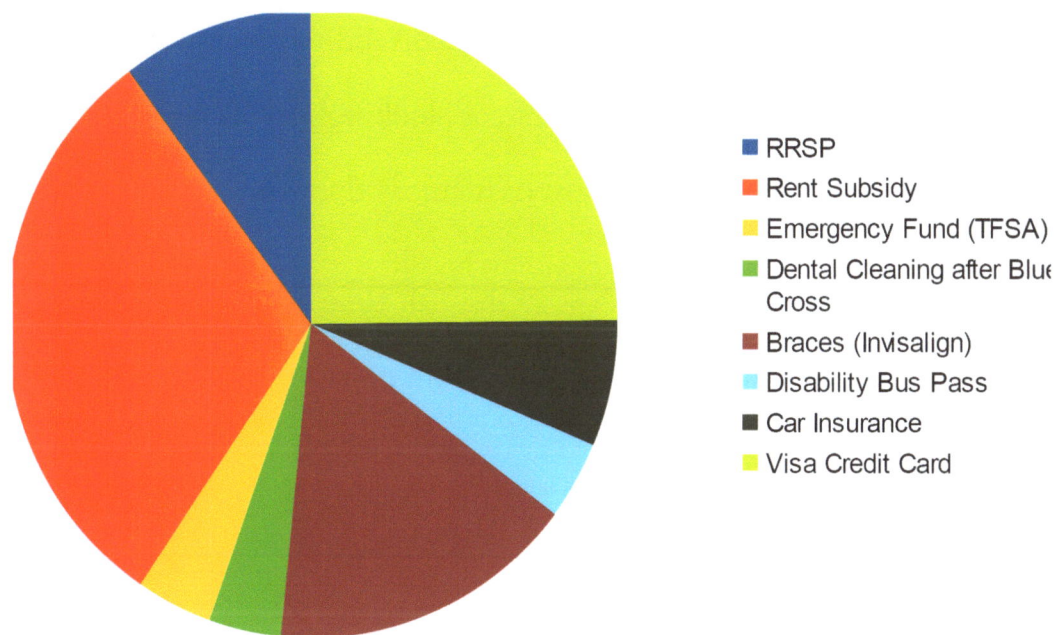

Rent Subsidy

So you can see here, Rent Subsidy is the largest portion of your budget. Before I got serious about savings, Rent was the first thing to come off my budget. But now I know I have to pay myself first!

Rent subsidies are hard to get now, but if you have one keep it. A rent subsidy means the company paying your rent will pay it in full to your landlord and in return you pay $375 to the said company.

Dental Cleaning after Blue Cross

Thankfully I pushed to get Blue Cross with PWD disability insurance. It paid off! I got my eyes checked for free, a subsidized paid of cool looking glasses, and dental insurance. My dentist is great, by the way. I find most of them shady.

I also got a secondary Blue Cross with working full time from home. There are many perks to working full time and getting benefits from most legit companies.

Braces (Invisalign)

My parents got my eldest sister braces and my younger brother braces, but not me and my other sister. Every birthday and Christmas I'd save all my brownie points and ask for braces, but nope.

And the funny thing is? My eldest sister had to get braces again because the first time didn't straighten her teeth. And my younger brother's teeth all fell out and had to get dentures. He is waiting for implants.

Luckily I didn't get braces with my parents and faced the consequences of poor orthodontic treatment. They told me to save my money and get them myself as an adult. And I have done that. $6230 for straightening my pearly whites. They said it's going to take 18 months with Invisalign. I chose Invisalign because I don't trust metal or plastic braces. Plus you can take them out when you eat.

Disability Bus Pass

I used to work for transit so I got a free pass through my work. It was great for 7 years, as I use buses and Skytrain all the time in Metro-Vancouver. And luckily I was part-time there so I had disability insurance as back-up. And disability insurance has $50/month unlimited pass.

Car Insurance

Luckily you can find cars under $1000 on Facebook and Craigslist. I budgeted and saved for 4 months to get a Yellow Ford Focus sports edition. Insurance is $160 so me and my partner go halfers so my portion is $80 per month. Luckily he's mechanical and smart so he can fix any problems on the car.

www.ingramcontent.com/pod-product-compliance
Lightning Source LLC
Chambersburg PA
CBHW051839210526
45473CB00005B/1943